Books by Neil Stanners

'Somewhere Night Falls' - Stories of childhood.

'Visions' - An exiled artist and an interesting family.

'The Magic Room' - Berlin 1945. Where do you hide from the Russians?

'The Knowing Room' - Sequel to The Magic Room. A journey with terrible truths.

'Assigned Climes' - Stories from the world in all its oddness and intrigue.

'The Horizon Tree' - The tricks and traps of knowing time.

In collaboration with Professor James Caspet -

'Lifeland' - An explanation of humans, our world and other matters.

Collector's Collection

LANDS

The Poetry of Neil Stanners

Published by Garamonde 2023

International distribution.
Copyright (Text and Covers)
Neil Stanners 2023

The moral right of the author has been asserted.

All rights reserved. No part of this book may be reproduced or transmitted in any form or by any means, electronic or mechanical, including photocopying, recording or by any information storage and retrieval system, without prior knowledge and permission in writing from the author.

ISBN 978-1-86275-019-7
Production by Media Services
Cover image - Neil Stanners

Preface

What is a poet? Not a question I had pondered until it was suggested I seek publication of my work. The answer is simple. A poet is a person who writes poetry.
On those grounds I meet the criteria.

Some poets are prolific, I am not.
Some poets are very good, some are bad. That is for the readers to judge.
Some poets achieve fame and become household names. A great many do not.
Of the many who do not, there are almost certainly some who are very good.
The world and the various forces that guide its decisions can be fickle. Powered by many interests there is not a lot that can be done by the 'poet'. You put your work out there and then wait a while to see if anybody notices your existence.

What about, greed, self-interest, marketing, talk shows, promotion of lesser talents
at the expense of others?
It's all true. (See page 77 of this book.) I have none of the aforementioned aids.
In the end I just need to find out.
So, here's my work. Written fleetingly over many years.
Read it out loud with appropriate timing and lustful projection. Use an accent that suits each work.
Mark the ones you like and read them to a friend. That's how the world goes round.

Note.
I am an author. I write books. You'll find a list of them near the front of this book.
Publishers like fiction. It potentially sells.
Poetry, not so much.
Prove them wrong.

Contents

Memories	9
In The Dark	10/11
Connections	12
From The Cliffs	13
Colours Of Blue	14
This Land	15
Off The Track	16/17
Already Gone	18
Boondoggle	19
Bus Stop	20/21
The Riverwood	22/23
Southern Winter Morning	24/25
A Taste	26
Big Boy	27
Crossing Holy Loch	28/29
The Man	30
Hokum Spokum	31-33
Jailyard Watch	34
The Academy	35
A Loss	36
Pause	38/39
Home Town Visit	40/41
Voyagers	42/43
Road To The Moon	44/45
Silence and Summer Heat	46/47
A Bush Clearing	48-51
Landfall	52/53
Softly	54/55
Skulkin'	56/57
Money - Gonna Get Me Some	58/59
Out In The World	60
One Of Us Is Leavin'	61
The Last Words Of Moorant	62/63
Autumn Morning Bayswater Road	64/65
Houses	66/67
Empty Road	68/69
Findin' My Way in The Blues	70
Layin' Low	71
A Protest	72
Speakenot	73
Sister Carey's Loss	74/75
A Life	76
Boldini	77
Photos	78/79
The Kid	80/81
The Other One	82/83
Learning	84
Knowledge	85
Dover Landing	86/87
The Poem	88/89
Yugoslavian Night	90
Time	91
Traveller's Tale	92/93
Beach	94/95
'Bot	96
Renewal	97
Black	98/99
Budawngs	100
Buying Time	101
The River and Me	102
First and Last	103
Meanings	104
Wisdom	105
End	106/107

Memories

These memories
These thoughts gone wild
Flooding in the mind
Taking down defences
Waking on the mood
        Sudden bursting rain

Holding up the day
Forgotten words
and hidden hopes
Lost lines
and odd old places
        Awkward back again

Gathered for a mixed assault
When defences are at ebb
Life and all its plans
Reminders of mortality
Other dust lost pieces
        Displayed then left for dead

In The Dark

In the dark, in the streets, in the depths of the night
When the day has gone far away
I'm always passing by, you can hear me in a sigh
    I never seem to stay too long

In the dark, by the moon, when sleep is in the room
And the world is an empty place
I'm the shadow on the wall, the distant train call
    The one who isn't there

In the dark out there I can sense some despair
I can hide in the dreams of a child
Take the sound in the night and make it alright
    Be gone before the light

In the dark let me be it's where I can see
I know my way from here
At the edge of the glade where the street light fades
    Just me passing by again

In the dark each night you can call me if you like
And I might answer your cry
I can't say I'll be your friend but maybe I can lend
    a little of my life for awhile.

This started as a song.
Oddly it connects with a lot of people.

Connections

Fish in the stream
    hawk on the hill
A line is drawn
    from the eye to the gill

From The Cliffs

A fair wind
      touches this plankton sea
      this saline scented sea
      brushes the swell
      and heads away
           like a demented dancer

      flinging spray

Moaning in the canyons
      brackish black canyons
      trailing out
      glassy walls
      hitting and angry
          childish temper

      resolving

A wet line
      shows their reach
      their limits
      beyond and above
      the cliffs remain
          haughty

      secure

Purposeful white
      wandering caps
      seeking purpose
      become an army
      speeding to battle
          hurling

      at our bastion

Where below the bodies of the vanquished

      cry and die.

Colours Of Blue

Green is the grass and there's the black night sky
Red is the colour of my grey cat's eye
The colour of my life it is clear and true
And the colour of my life that colour is blue

The brown skinned girl with her black-eyed boy
And yellow is the colour of that pull-along toy
The colours of my life ain't nuthin' new
The same dark shade, that colour is blue.

The gold of the morn and park's autumn trees
Empty brown paths where you go as you please
The colour of the hole where you buried me
Blue and dark and nobody can see

Some colours are bright and others are dull
Dark as the shadows in the eyes of a skull
The colours in my days since losing you
Take me to the edge where the nights are so blue.

This Land

Took this road through the land
This land through my life
A long star-filled night that led to the light
Took it all of the way through the days of my past
This land of my soul, this road to my heart

Take it back, take it back
And follow it home
Back to the child that you knew
And find your way home through the mists of the fields
To the place where you dwelt long ago

And you'll know of the time
In the depths of your mind
When peace flowed over you
It fell to your arms in those new hungry charms
This land where you grew to the day

The seas and the skies
The waste of goodbyes
The taste of the new
This world shining through

Took this road through the land
This land through my life
A long star-filled night that led to the light
Took it all of the way through the days of my past
This land of my soul, this road to my heart

If I ever had to write an anthem,
this would be it.

Off The Track

If I take this way
        on rock and soil
Where even the trees
        are older than me

And never
        pass this way again

I will still have been here
        for a moment
Where time has known an age
        before we came

And so it will be
        when we have moved on

Already Gone

You can't catch the train if the train's left the station
Can't get no whisky from an empty jar
    Can't hear the music less you turn it on
    You can't hold your baby if she's already gone.

You can't have no fight if there ain't no opponent
Can't collect the money if you didn't bet
    Can't hear the music less you turn it on
    You can't hold your baby if she's already gone.

You can't have no journey less you take the first step
Can't smoke cigars with a cigarette
    Can't hear the music less you turn it on
    You can't hold your baby if she's already gone.

You can't hold the flowers that you didn't pick
You can't play guitar less you know a good lick
    Can't hear the music less you turn it on
    You can't hold your baby if she's already gone.

You can't bake pie less you got the right meat
Can't pass that test less you know how to cheat
    Can't hear the music less you turn it on
    You can't hold your baby if she's already gone.

Can't be somebody till you learn how to give
You can't have a life if you haven't lived
    Can't hear the music less you turn it on
    You can't hold your baby if she's already gone.

Boondoggle

Boondoggle now dog and a bone
Boondoggle now dog and a bone
Gonna get ya gonna find ya real soon
Like a Boondoggle dog and a bone
You can't do that   Gonna take it back
Boondoggle now I'm on your track

Boondoggle now dog and a bone
Seeking you out hiding under the moon
You gettin' away but not so far
Got ways of knowing where you are
Take it back   You know it's mine
Boondoggle its a nasty crime

Boondoggle people say I'm mad
Boondoggle yeh I got it bad
No respect for people like you
When you think you safe I say peekaboo
You done what you done   Now you better run
Boondoggle I could be anyone

Boondoggle now dog and a bone
Boondoggle now dog and a bone
Hey hey I'm just down the road
Like a Boondoggle dog and a bone
I can smell your sweat   I can feel your fear
Boondoggle I'm almost here

Boondoggle now can you see
Look in the crowd - which one is me?

A Boondoggle is a small useless item often made of leather.
Or could it be the name of your pursuer.

Bus Stop

We waited together
        spaced on the bench
The bus due
        soon
Old and young
        alone

He looked at me
        quizically
I smiled back
        gently
Took some initiative
        "How are you?"

He looked again
        sadly it seemed
"I'm overwhelmed."
        "How so?"
"By memories."
        he sighed

"Are they good
        or bad?"
"They are all
        so many.
A burden of life
        and age."

The bus appeared
        rolling along
Time was
        drawing short
"Give some to me,"
        I said

He looked with kindness
        rarely seen
I lifted my small hand
        to his
"This is not my bus.
        Hurry please."

He held out his hand
        to mine
Held tight for quite
        some moments
Then he had
        to board

As the 912 pulled
        away
From the window he
        caught my eye
"Thank you."
        he made to say

I have them now
        I keep them safe
Added all
        to mine
Neat and new and
        all in a line

The Riverwood

I met the girl alone and hot
Down in the river wood
We both knew what we liked a lot
Down in the river wood
The dark trees and the shadowed breeze
Down in the river wood
There it was we did those deeds
Down in the river wood

She said to me you know its bad
Down in the river wood
The man he knows I wander here
Down in the river wood
He has a gun, he has no fear
Down in the river wood
The paths we tread, be careful here
Down in the river wood

In that summer's heat we met once more
Down in the river wood
And stole away where the light is poor
Down in the river wood
We heard him move, we saw the flash
Down in the river wood
He fell and died and left us there
Down in the river wood

Now the child we made that day
Down in the river wood
Seeks the trees with barefoot ease
Down in the river wood
In time he knows there'll be that day
Down in the river wood
When a girl will wander in to play
Down in the river wood
There eyes will meet and they will stay
Down in the river wood

It's dark and green and magic there
Down in the river wood
If you wait and hold your breath
Down in the river wood
Then something joins your soul for you
Down in the river wood
And time is still and silence falls
Down in the river wood
For those that know and care to go
Down in the river wood

Southern Winter Morning

It's early
    alone
white mist
    makes the world small

        dog barking
        from somewhere
        a muffled mutt

my voice floats
    nobody to hear
    this early hour

        shoes and sounds
        magnified
        close to oneself

            this day
            it's empty
            I'm wrapped and waiting

                the pines
                drip - remind me
                of Germanic climes

                    misplaced - like me
                    at this
                    country railway

A Taste

At rare times
In the very early
      light of day
I taste for an instant
      the like of all possession
      of this soul we hold

Could be the soul
      is of our making?

But the taste lingers

Big Boy

Got some big boy lovin' gonna give it away
Got a lot a moves you won't see round this way
All night long an' all day too
Come on now it's waitin' for you
Line up ladies take a look at me
I'm the finest damn thing that you ever did see

You see me in the south an' you see me in the west
Lotta ladies happy 'cause I is the best
Tickle your fancy an' tidy your drawers
With my super skills I tend to my chores
Line up girls now take a look and see
I'm pretty an' I'm good - You just can't let me be

Bop bop Baba   ba ba   ba ba
Bop bop Baba   ba ba   ba ba
Dee dee deedee   deedle e dee
Finest damn thing that you ever did see

Crossing Holy Loch

That morning on the Loch
As we crossed away
from the little grey town
it was lady of our night
where our thoughts most lay

A whisper of a woman
an old and gentle Scot
Giving up her bed
insisting that we eat
for the few bob we could afford

In her parlour
she gazed upon the floor
as she spoke of fearsome bombers
hurtling down the Loch
to kill her husband at their door

We talked till all we had was said
Our figures in the darkening room
became points to aim a voice
But light would spoil the moment
the sadness in the gloom

Morning was departure
We were slow to go
In reluctance we hugged the lady
who treated us as sons
So little did we know

Silent on the railings
watching water slipping by
a day in two young lives
of learning the world of woes
Oh how our years would fly

Young and exploring the world looking
for somewhere to spend the night.
A local copper directed us to her house
overlooking the Loch.

The Man

I was out walking on this endless road
Chasing each day trying to lighten my load
Taking my time and leading nowhere in between

A man came from a field and he said to me
I can see in your eyes you just want to be free
But you don't know how or where or which way to go

    So you gotta keep on travellin' on
    Lookin' for somewhere that you can belong
    Never pass a chance and never let it go too long

I kept him in mind as I went on my way
Over each hill to greet the new day
Lookin' for the place that time would tell me to stay

I met him again some years ago
A little worn down with nothing to show
The man I knew, that man I saw was me

    So now I keep on travellin' on
    Lookin' for somewhere that I can belong
    I never pass a chance and never let it go too long

Yeh I never pass a chance
    and never let it go too long

'Hokum Skokum'

Hokum Skokum

Hokum Lokum
The kids are loose
Lokum Skokum
The kids are loose
Speak no sound. There'll be no truce
The kids are out. The kids are loose.

They're not the same. They're not to know
They creep at the door
And low on the path
Slide in the trees
And call from the moor
They're there, they're there, they're loose

Hokum Lokum
Say it twice
Lokum Skokum
Say it thrice
Let them know, let them hear
Do not fear or shed no tear

They're smart, they're sly
I tell no lie
Do not believe
Look not their eye
They get, they hold
They grow no old

Hokum Lokum
The kids are loose
Lokum Skokum
The kids are loose
Hope the best and say no worst
The kids are out. The kids are loose.

I've met quite a few kids.
For a while they're odd and interesting.
Then they grow up and the oddness goes away.

Jailyard Watch

The devils in the detail in this jailhouse yard
Boys have got me lookin' round lookin' real hard
Don't know what they doin' an' thinkin' about
Stayin' out of the corners stayin' out of the dark
Gotta get goin' - get back in the line
      Devils walkin' with me now - its gonna be fine

Down in the cells in this corner block
Hear the boys talkin', talkin' a lot
They got somethin' goin' on in their mind
Sayin' somthin' 'bout somebody lyin'
Don't eat the food an' sleep with one eye
      Devils sleepin' side me so it oughta be fine

Made it to mornin' and it's grey and alone
Guards are goin' crazy 'cause a body's been found
Nobody seen and nobody heard
I settled that somethin' now I'm free as a bird
Relax in the yard, space is all mine
      Devils sittin' with me here its gonna be fine

      Devils in the detail in this jailhouse yard

Recorded this song some years ago.
Our CD sold well.
But yesterday's gone.

The Academy

Chords await the careless
        where music trips the soul
in the academy
of sound

Only those who know
        the password
ever go
within

The walls
        are bare
inside
there

No one to ask
        the word
to aid
return

The line
        is on the lips
of those
who wait anew

A Loss

You may not know the reason why -
or care to
but I am with you still
in the world you knew
Examining each day as it comes
My life seems a pursuit
of the place where time has taken you

Are you aware -
that I wander these days
with silly hope?
Or would you have me view the earth
with more indifferent eyes
from a new less troubled
point of view

Written for a friend in a time of grief.
I hope it helped.

Pause

In Paris - stranded by language
Far north of the shaped feelings
   that have lined my life
There in a shop of brusque gallic fare
with coffee, bread and sweet tarts -
I can smell eucalypts?
As clear and clean waisted
as rain on, heat haunted
forests of the tablelands

Meshed, netted and racked -
   frozen at their table
Cup poised, in the proprietor's eye
(working on spittle within his moustache)
My words, his words
Could make no sense of these dark
pointed leaves
that have unburdened their scent
in a brass railed nook
off the Boul' Mich'

A moment, flicked, flittering away
   back to this day
To the dappled sun
of their rich, green softworld
of filtered light
The proprietor's eye moves on
His coffee invades and pervades
fat vowels of their native tongue
But I had it, they did not

Home Town Visit

I am from the future
Nobody has noticed me
    standing here
Despite my mature pose
They seem not
    to know

With every rolling second
Presenting a new
    direction
(or endless alternatives)
I have arrived at this
    point

And through the changes
It is all around me -
    waiting
The miracle of moments
That cry for attention
    Yet cannot be explained.

All the ages, the places
The times that have seen
    my passing
Have not held my sway
to return in regret
    this day

I can look - now
See the childhood
    that rushed by
Here - in reflection
Time to regret that
    I let it die

Voyagers

But I have known
have faced alone
kept company with
the light of time
and all its destinations

Would but one second
be the hour
the moment of discovery
when all the senses have
run out

And freely
touched by uplifting hands
roll and float
travel with impunity
to invented lands

Bound not by body
held down by flesh and bones
with just the spirit left
stepped off
and slipped away

To cry out
in empty halls
to friends and others
and scatter to stars
in endless space

Road To The Moon

I been this way before
I been this way before
Walkin' through the night when the sky is clear
Nobody sees an' nobody hears
Quietly whistlin' an ol' time tune
Seems like there's a road to the moon

I seen this road before
I seen this road before
Got me some bread from a window sill
Hid by the trees while I got my fill
That silvery streak through the scent of the blooms
Seems like there's a road to the moon

I walked these hills before
I walked these hills before
The cool night air is soft an' free
Better than the heat of the day you see
Make it to the top of the ridge real soon
Seems like there's a road to the moon

I been everywhere before
I been everywhere before
Get so tired I just don't know
My lady loves gone, she'll never show
There's one place yet I've got to go
I'll take the road to the moon

Yeh, There's one place yet I've got to go

I'll take the road to the moon

Silence and Summer Heat

It is a smooth flat rock
        on which to rest
A rarity in this wilderness
        of tangled growth and trees

I had companions once
        to tread these dark unknowns
They are no more these days
        so now I walk alone

Somewhere on this rare lost track
        more a hint than a way
Waiting for inspired thoughts
        lest I go astray

It creeps and skulks
        makes you aware
Tiny moves and landscape crackles
        hot and bold and bare

Would they find my bones
        left behind this rock?
Consult the map that is no help
        use instincts I keep in stock

Is it amused
        this hopeless growth
Surrounding me and bearing
        heat and little caring

Now I'm up and have my pack
        weighing on my back and mind
There was an in at the start
        just the out to find

'A Bush Clearing'

'A Bush Clearing'

A Bush Clearing

At the end of the day - losing light
   A space where none should be
Open and familiar
waiting

Somehow - the tree was always there
   It seemed alone, out of place
As if a table setting
in the ferns

Cleared back - a good distance
   An unsettling feeling
That's what gave the secret up
A vine on the foreign tree

Then there was the stone
   Stacked upon stone
Even the hole
where they kept the kettle

It felt warm - familiar
   As best I could tell
They made children (poor dumb buggers with no future)
right here where I stood

It seemed about right
   In a one-roomed hut
The bed would - be positioned
near the fire

And they ate
   by this window
With a view of the hill
where the children are

People who trek through the Australian bush will sometimes find a few odd trees or plants and an old clearing. Pioneers always built the home fireplace and chimney of stone. Often they are the only remaining clue that once people lived right here.

Landfall

What made this landfall
before our time
Scraped its prow
beached its craft
To stand still
within the shadow of the trees
listening for sounds beyond
natures stirrings

Those that would tell
not of a weary specious humanity
but reveal perhaps
a greater gift
of new and exotic structure
noble and assured
To greet and exchange
the coming

Within the creature
moving forward
stood a longing
a double strength
to plant the muscle
but dwelled the knowledge
of a foot on a distant land
and the fame of its tale

Therein lay the key
in these dark eccentric pasts
to reward to riches
to gratitude
illuminating the masses
expanding possession
marking maps
beyond horizons

Stretching an arm
to touch leaves
dew wet
unhurried by the sun
Shadows like a poultice
draw him on
passing through the matted
green persistent foliage

Seeking a sign
that a flag may rise
a proclamation
be made
on this splendid group
These lands
of promise
on a vast new sea

To join in celebration
ancient noble places
of fire and fable
wrought of steel
and grapeshot
Fashioned by great
imperial might
and fine causes

Upon a hill
past the beach
heads line in view
observing the clippers
rise and fall
and those that came
from within
to enter uninvited

A shaft
of selected forest wood
sharpened on stone
and hardened in fire
seeks out the figures
standing there
to die like a vipers strike
silently

Back they hurry
back his mortal retreat
lacking the elegance
of his advance
Again upon the water
staring as they row
at hurried footprints
his own - and nothing more

Above
the towering greenery
twisted at defiant tropic will
stares back - arms folded
at the matchwood craft
in the coral quay below
To which it will return
with guns

Softly

Softly - I'm calling you to my door
Softly - I'm calling you to my door
The moon is dull the light is poor
Can't see a rabbit or the line of the shore
Callin' your name - watchin' the cabin door

Callin' your name, watchin' the shadows fall
Callin' your name, watchin' the shadows fall
I hear your dress against the wind
Your feet are treadin', this doll is pinned
Callin' your name, watchin' the shadows fall

Callin' your name, I know you're gettin' near
Callin' your name, I know you're gettin' near
The trees now still, you move in fear
You walk in a dream, you're almost here
The cabin door is open now my dear

The cabin door is open now my dear

Also a song.
Played in a minor key with suitable breathless vocals it evokes the dangers of veturing into the swampland alone.

Skulkin'

There's   the man   the man I gotta see
There's   that man   he's walkin' in front o' me
There's   the man   the man I'm gonna see
He's   the one   who did those wrongs to me

I got the gun and I got the knife
Gonna be some alterations to life

With   that man   who's just up ahead o' me.
Yeh   the man   gettin' visitations from me

There's   the woman   the woman I gotta see
There's   that woman   she's walkin' in front o' me
With   the man   the man I'm gonna see
They's   the ones   who did those wrongs to me

I got the knife and I got the gun
What I plan ain't gonna be fun

With   that pair   who's just up ahead o' me
Yeh   those two   gettin' visitations from me

So   I know   I know what I gotta do
Yeh   I know   I know who I'm doin' it to
They're   the ones   whos' goin' to know
Just   how far   I'm goin' to go

I got the knife, the gun an' the means
Life won't be as good as it seems

For   that pair   who's just up ahead o' me
Yeh   those two   gettin' visitations from me

So   I know   I know what I gotta do
Yeh   I know   I know who I'm doin' it to
They're   the ones   whos' goin' to know
Just   how far   I'm goin' to go

I got the knife, the gun an' the means
Life won't be as good as it seems

For   that pair   who's just up ahead o' me.
Yeh   those two   gettin' visitations from me

This started and continues as a song. It has a strict rhythm. The bass line and drums beats hold it together. Tap your fingers and put in the pauses as you read.

Money Gonna Get Me Some

I like pretty girls who like diamonds and pearls
And money's gonna get me some

And money's gonna get me some

I like fast new cars and funky bars
And the girls all gather around

And money's gonna get me some

I like deep gold mines and rare french wines
And the girls who drink it down

And money's gonna get me some

Tell 'em you're poor and it's love you adore
Sing 'em your poems and your songs
Get 'em to weep but that mountain's too steep
No money an' you're gonna get none

So give me big white yachts to sail out where it's hot
And the girls all dance in the night

And money's gonna get me some

See it's why I like pretty girls who like diamonds and pearls
And money's gonna get me some

Yeh money's gonna get me some

Out In The World

Thinkin' of you babe, out in the world
Stormin' each town with yo flag unfurled
Catfish cunnin' an' alligator shoes
What in God's name you think you do
Gonna fall down, it's gonna be far

Meet you at the bottom in some ten-cent bar

Say can you see from the top this hill
It's a long long way back an' it's a long way still
Followin' your trail, it ain't real hard
I can see the signs in every man's yard
Gonna fall down, it's gonna be far

Meet you at the bottom in some ten-cent bar

Lookin' for you babe, enjoyin' the laugh
Admire it all, don't do things by half
Twenty men now lookin' for your blood
Chasin' all day through the heat and the mud
Gonna fall down, it's gonna be far

Meet you at the bottom in some ten-cent bar

One Of Us Is Leavin'

Lovin' you is like an endless war
I want my life like it was before
Not busted all over the floor
Young an' fresh an' let's do it some more
Ain't worth the trouble, the mess and the pain.
One of us is leavin' on the midnight train.

We met too young, too safe and too clean
Couldn't stay apart, you know what I mean
Then the lovin' started gettin' extreme
I'm only one man babe an' you need a team
Now you put on warpaint an' dance in the rain
One of us is leavin' on the midnight train.

Oh now honey I love you when you mad
Don't get down low an' look so sad
We can work on it a little and work on it a lot
That paint an' those tears make you look so hot
Say what you doin' now is drivin' me insane
An' if we hurry you can still catch that train

The Last Words Of Moorant

"I look at the dictators and despots
        lords of industry, the champions and the heroes
        all those religious masters, the famous and infamous,
        the many giant egos of humanity
        as they come and they go ....

Then I look up at the universe

How incredibly tiny we are."

From my book 'The Horizon Tree'.

Autumn Morning Bayswater Road

Hands in a heavy coat
Bayswater Road in the new light
Of a Sunday before the world rises
Fuzzy in the dew drawn white
Of not quite falling rain

A last yellow staining street lamp
Departs the grey dawn
In silent retreat
Leaving this motionless avenue
Of sodden leaves

These trees beside Hyde Park
Catch my breath
From an upturned head down collar
Their old fingers examining
The texture I expel

Heading home
To the flat - tea and toast
Beside the bed before rest
Exhausted sleep at sunrise
The night people give way to the day

On Bayswater Road there are shoppers
And painters and potters
And ice cream machines
A crazy foreign London land
In my midday wandering dreams

Houses

I loved their houses
They were rich and had two
Their son befriended me
I know not why
Perhaps to start a collection
like a pinned butterfly

Their house on the hill
had a courtyard
you entered through an arch
It surrounded you
bringing privacy and protection
Like a prison

You're my friend, he said
as if I had been labelled
They provided food and
entertainment
In a careless lazy manner
of those who have it all

The beach house
was timber with balconies
Newly old, salty, sandy
and opulent
We played in the surf and I
rescued their son

His father was angry
I should have left him
He had to learn
Perhaps death in the pusuit
of wealth
are somehow connected

Visits continued
I was owned and displayed
This is Nigel's 'friend'
Comfortable and pampered
Used as a measure
of their boy

Integrated and free
to wander in and
be part of their world
Secretly enjoying their
houses and
architecture

Christmas came
My parents said I should
accept their invitation and
take a present
I attended presentless
How could I compete

They gave me something
magnificent
Their boy meanwhile
had so much more
A wondeful day
till the end

Throats were cleared and
silence fell
Glances went about
It seemed all warmth
had left the room
As a message came right out

Their son, they said
would be at a new and different
school next year
He would not be able to
accommodate me
anymore

I loved their houses
They were rich and had two

Dusty Road

Dusty road, hello again
How you bin, my old friend

Seems a while since I bin here
Say at least this time last year

Know you don't lead anywhere
Where I'm goin', that place is there

So take me in your arms once more
Show me all I'm lookin' for

Silent fields and empty skies
Long lost words and lone bird cries

The still, slow days, the darkest nights
Let me see if there's a light

I'm weary now, I'd like to sleep
Please turn away, if I should weep

Dusty road, hello again
I'm with you now until the end.

Findin' My Way In The Blues

It's a dark ol' street - there's a chill in the air
Late in the night - there's nobody there
Corner light - is flickering slow
Goin' my way - with nowhere to go
I'm finding my way - in the blues

There's music somewhere - but a can't find the sound
There's no words to say - or be written on down
Take the corner - left or the right
Little by little - I'm all out of sight
I'm finding my way in the blues

I'm a struggling man - lost my woman and child
Too much liquor - an' goin' half wild
Had a bad stupid life - wrong side of the law
Nobody cares -   'bout me anymore

Where I go from here - just don't know
Can't get any lower - low as you go
Can't call out my sorrows - just no one to tell

Whole of the world - would see me in hell
I'm finding my way in the blues

Ongoing riff -
E   slide B (7)   D-G (5)   E (7)
A   slide E (7)   G-C (5)   A (7

Layin' Low

I'm takin' the train
I'm takin the bus
Walkin' for hours
In the rain and the dust
Takin' my time, takin' it slow
Till I get where I wanna go

Got me a ride
Fella in a truck
Says looks to me
Like you're down on your luck
You better believe, you better know how
Things, can only get better from now.

Goin' back down there
In the southern zone
Gettin' closer each day
Gonna find my way home
Then you'll see, ah then you'll know
Man in there is layin' low

There she is now
Way down by the river
Lonely an' tired
Got some mem'ries to give her
Takin' my time, fixin' her up
Just me an' some mongrel dog's pup

A Protest

You men of taste
and those of breeding
do you ever ask of the earth
inquire to its feeling

Wonder at the stars
touch and know a tree
see the land and love it
find a tear in what you see

Or are you blind
does deafness haunt your day
is to be aware of life
beyond your words to say

There is progress
and wealth and much to do
with little time to spare
the moments so few

You cannot know all of earth
this planet gives to you
the stage to strut and pose
and asks no call on what you do

Lust for power and more
is another human trait so
check the land on which you stand
and make a balanced state

Despite our many forms
nor whereabout we roam
abiding truth embraces all
we have but just one home

Speakenot

They did see batary goug
mafaray cray and
actal lan all at sea
and lost in weeds of moog

Treacher filled their tobal
aches of knowing noug
mobaya menturus mobaya milos
they cried in fits of loog

Lookana Lookana
Terrina jagus
Mobila goug
   Tantala ferokus

Ganay the sea
obelis saviourus
land now by noug
away from the moog

Ah, tis all makaras and lasas
that fortuna came
wence by the noug
fretanas not to lay to magar

So call and vocalus
maragar exultar
to defendal thay goug
enday they moog

Lookana Lookana
Terrina jagus
Mobila goug
   Tantala ferokus

Sometimes there's not a language that suits the purpose so a new one must be installed..

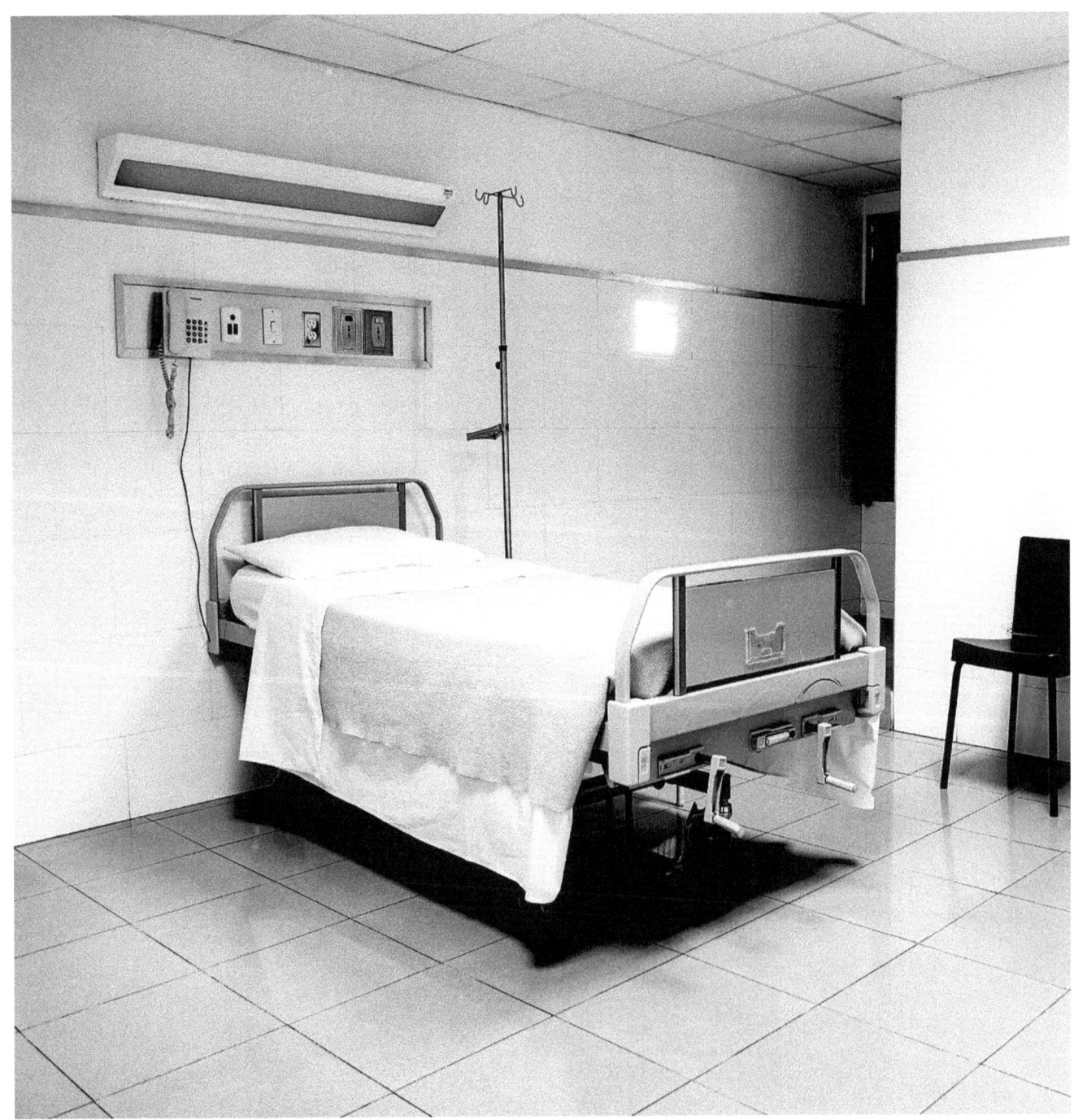

Sister Carey's Loss

He had fought for weeks
Chest heaving, eyes lined
this child of nine

Fingers grasping, seeking
Well made limbs
that circled the sheets

His carer would not see
him go
Not while she could run the show

He saw perhaps
just whiteness and gloom
Those watching had to assume

They sought responses
His a whimpered solitude which
fell in time to just a mood

The clear and fragile skin
Gave way on hands too small
to hold life in

She carried him down
the bannister stairs
Help was met with glares

Held him tight
wrapped and sewn
his final journey not alone

A hard woman
one to fear
but in the shadows there was a tear

Working the night shift for a while in a London Children's hospital I witnessed the nursing staff's anger and frustration at losing a child in their care.

A Life

It is a place
in this confusing cosmos
whereby life begins
   produces cells
   gathers memories
   exists
Then does not

It happens often
throughout the world
and no doubt others
   that this living occurs
   all in time
   noting observing being
Holding so much

Then it is gone
all this wealth
this magic
   the unique story
   talents and events
   are lost
Thus we are poorer

And so we dream
and so we die
to go unnoticed
   passing by
   a flicker a hint
   into the wilderness
With all the others

Boldini

There was a man
with three dogs ....
wrote Boldini
staring at the crucifix
upon his wall
for inspiration

Boldini was a writer
working as a cook
to support his secret passion
Living in the hope
that soon he would be
published and all would be as it should

Though of course it never
would ....
Boldini had much talent
but not the connections
And what is life
without connections

Still he lived in hope
For what have we left - if not hope

Photos

I have grown old
It happened tonight
(when I should have been doing
something constructive)
But the weather was cold

By the heater
lazy and alone
The book of photos looked faded
"These prints have lost their tone"
My wife smiled - in the pictures

Page by page - so so many
If I could have flicked them
under my thumb
A life would have hurried by
Less painful and numb

"I have grown old"
"God, she was pretty"
I am losing a game
I do not wish to play
It is the afternoon of the day

Well over half my share
Slipped away to God knows where
I miss her smile
Now I see

    that it is gone

The Kid

I know this kid
I know his ways
The thoughts he thinks
The games he plays

We met at first
some years before
He was smaller
and not so sure

But he improved
And learned and grew
I watched and waited
as more he knew

Now he moves
and carries forward
with some parts of me
all onboard

We were one
and all was fine
I didn't look
down the line

Yearly on
his change ensues
theres more of him
that now endures

We are parting
He is his own
Theres little to say
and none to own

Progress is loss
Time is a thief
breaking the bonds
held too brief

I knew this kid
I knew his ways
Now he's a stranger
who no longer plays

The Other One

This one is different
this girl
Unknown and
diffident

A careful path
to tread
To be sure
of what is said

A little thing
sensitive
And full of
spring

Haughty at times
but kind
Quiet and reflective
of mind

Needing assurance
more love
As with a soft
dove

I see how
these girls
are like
that

She grew
as they do
Had talents
and wishes

Looked
for answers
to questions
unasked

Settled now
away and remote
It's rare that we
even talk

We're friends
it's okay
but the little
girl's gone away

Learning

Many times before and
many times again
there's all I know
and that to come
stray lights of subtlety that
have/will be missed
broad strokes lain deep who
by their enormous presence
will be part of me

being as I am
a particle of life the
sore battered body

        of experience
that is
        just one
of all
        of us

Knowledge

Black black waters rippled home
at the end of an endless sea
Upon the grey-walled timeless shore
A man cried, "Pity me -
All the knowledge there is to know
is mine through eternity."

He looked about the wild-eyed waters
as waves lapped at his feet
Beneath his threaded ancient cloak
his cold sad heart did leak
Again he cried to faceless Gods
"I live to hear you speak."

Alone against an ink black sky
crouching in beaten retreat
He heard the moaning wind reply
as rain excused his tears
One to whom all is knowing is shown
cannot ever die

At the end of this endless sea
where the black waters rise
The grey walls sit and shield this man
Who waits
and knows the curse of knowing all
in that he will never be free

Dover Landing

In Dover we kissed the wharf
at 1am of a new day
Looked in dark shops
with signs we could read
and food
we could not afford

Met two girls barely fourteen
Who told us in easy english
of truckies they'd known
and places
they'd lain
Too cold to try their fare

Drank German Brandy
Ted had Rye Whisky
from an Army base in Soest
Warming our stomachs
hearts and minds
The girls could put it away

Huddled together
a warm little group
We started a drunken song
So the cops picked us up
kept hold of the girls
and told us to be on our way

Walked in the dark
not daunted by fate
Found a good fellow awake
A room for the night
Why not
No mention of being broke

Morning and breakfast
then cashed a cheque
Ted had held dog-eared for months
I bought a pork pie
We both said goodbye
to the castle on the hill

Out on our way
London bound
A lorryman gave us a lift
Then left the road
while checking his load
We ricocheted of a tree

Disgorged in the snow
after two somesaults
Ted said - Hell, did we die?
I looked at my blood
bright and red
Not sure I returned his cry

We took photos like tourists
I lived
We left the driver alone
Hitching again
I said to my friend
It's really good to be home?

Actual events. The midnight ferry from Calais after many months of wandering round Europe.

Sweet Justice —
enabled
too easy to trouble
far
Elegant with mind
over machinery,
all of us stay
A chorus of wanting (waiting?)
with
no means to pay.

The chaos of
on
thy blue facade. go!!

False-heed my
intention invention
forsakes all about

When laws are about
but these
human lost out.

The Poem

Now -
immortalised in this glass case
                just something
he scribbled down
                one day
that took hold
                became a part
reproduced these many
                years

The pieces
the words
                their connection in rhyme
so natural then
                scarcely noticed by time
written jerkily
                on a train
on rails
                line by line

It speaks of love
of hope
                life with all its
complexities
                seen by one who
could see
                and look above
yet angered by
                mortality

The pen beside
the yellow page
                passed over
by a careless age
                withstanding our
tormenting
                brief pause
each stroke of the pen
                the world he adored

Yugoslavian Night

Prostate in a tent
Flapping mountain cold
Between earth and skin
a plastic sheet moulding the rocks

I have no spare clothes
I wear them all
To no avail
against this fabric piercing chill

Hoping for dawn
To end the tormented night
As a hint of grey reveals
a search for wood on this barren slope

Brandy to warm me
Producing a headache
A body to warm me
not now to know

Sleep   dawn   a fire
Smoky soup flowing well being
Within and without
standing for bones to crack

Wind ruffling across the view
Striking silence in our quartet
Over the valley
a sound of sheep bells

It is a day with promise

Nobody speaks against the night

Long ago and far away it seems like only yesterday. Some memories stick I know not why. Perhaps to reassure me that there was light in other days.

Time

Be ready
prepare
when your children
turn into foreigners
there is
no one else there

Age is transient
no moment secure
the pace
the promise
you're caught in
the lure

Take time
divide
apportion the pieces
Give each nothing more
as the shadow
increases

The task
is to be
in each moment
and then
move on and away
as the stroke of a pen

The Traveller's Tale

Brush away the shadows, carry off the light.
Hold onto the darkness, travel through the night.
Take the lost and lonely, keep the end in sight.

Roads and hills and rivers, land that lays out bare
Press against the trailing wind, go on if you dare
Twenty all times twenty, find a way to there

Time is not your master, time is not your friend
All across the wicked ways, all around each bend
Call out still into the night, can you see the end

Are you running, are you winning?
Are you lost or found?
All those doubts and all those sounds.

Taking all the paths you find and never know the way
Lost alone its all the same, come the newest day
Not a line of verse to say in this endless play

Are you running, are you winning?
Are you lost or found?
All those doubts and all those sounds.

Beach

It is wise
This day that is slow
    drawn on heat soft
    water light summer
    green eyes

It is brown
With salt-burned limbs
long-lidded lifting sand
    lain lengthways
    to the sun

It is pure
As crusted bread
    with softed soul
    awaiting knowing
    upon the shelf

It is brave
As stone and lizard
    helpless drug dreamed
    azure white capped bliss
    on the yellow white expanse

It is tomorrow
In an angular sure
    crucifix pose
    a raw-boned near naked
    prey of time

It is uncaring
Unknowing its power
    where youth exists
    the fleeting hours
    go misundertsood

The lone languid figure of a girl enjoying peace and sunshine on an empty beach.

'Bot

I spoke today
to one of them
Building learning
knowing their ways

If they are new
to you
Take Care
Beware

Meet their eyes
Know what is true
They have a power
unknown to you

We stood alone
its face benign
A summary of mystery
I could not define

Should I speak
or wait
The Laws are vague
of late

Was it a time
to let it know?
We are as one
and let it go

Then it spoke
with words I knew
Simply now
I am 74682

I had the key
I knew the code
I was aware
In the mode

This thing before
flesh and bone
A human life
setting the tone

Await its order
Obey its wit
How easy would be
to finish it

Renewal

Yet when it is all
and all we have become
To change now what is done
take away the knowing -
Give fate another run

That labour of will
drawing hard each breath
Seek the summit take the hop
Where it is - that view
can only be seen from the top

Living with our guilts
and our triumphs alike
(One is much the other)
Consider tastes and time
the blunt the nil the spike

Having reached your height
of which there is no other
With wind and lift rushing on
Wear your hopes on your back
step forward and then step off

Black

If the darkness didn't end
at the end of the dakened corridor
The groping corner turned
does not reveal a light

Awash in a sea of shapeless black
cast away by uncertainty
Here lies lost and frailty
as no hint comes to life

Eyes are taken out
by lack of their neccessity
Nothing to receive
no contact for their use

To feel around in shapeless haste
for semblence of shape
Listen wave and look
at the nothingness about

Then lost you are
as those cautious souls
White caned world is yours
as others robbed before

Dormant fear now rises
to swing ever wild your limbs
Is this your lot your new
approach without a hope

Ever on your quest
as panic hurries forth
No line no reason
now ensures your path

It comes as if by accident
a hint a drip a glimmer
A tiny spot of precious form
the guide to the dilemma

As forward you move
as steps you make
All is calm is sense
and all the dark forgiven

Budawangs

Mass of rumpled rock
powered by earthen history
held by forest density
defiant to intrusion
a beast of vast illusion

East of the coast with
lofts of hopeless heights
tight gullies hidden valleys
castles creeks and domes
this mix of wary sights

Known by the dark men
revered in their stories
eons of waiting
pagodas and green rooms
some lost some doomed

A range of worn-down massifs
determined by time
brooding holding their sway
watching entry and exit
waiting out the day

Secret holder trickster of fate
standing in silent wait
until it is too late
it is all here in these
cathedrals of the wild

The Budawangs are a southern part of the Great Dividing Range that runs down most of the east coast of Australia. They are beautiful, rugged and unforgiving.

Buying Time

I want to buy some time my friend
Where do you shop for a day or two
I want to buy some time today
Spend it all on you

Walk the streets of the town I knew
In the light of an autumn moon
Stand and look and know it all
Come the day they'd wake up soon

Take a bus on a special road
To the river on a summer day
Meet my buddies at ten years old
When we come out to play

I want the day when we first met
To see your eyes again
To fix that life already set
You cant leave me alone

So
I want to buy some time my friend
Where do you shop for a day or two
I want to buy some time today
And spend it seeing you

The River and Me

I followed the river
talked to its flow
heard gurgled answers
to things I should know

Kept to the bank
eased by my tread
just me and the river
Do you know me? I said

I've waited for you
it calmly replied
for this day, this hour
when you would arrive

We have but a moment
before its too late
alone and together
a sample of fate

I walked on for hours
in the empty bushland
just me and this river
so close at hand

We discussed many things
in a scholarly way
So much at ease
and so much to say

My unease now eased
my doubts assuaged
My friend the river
and me on our stage

It led me on
this watery trail
heard my feelings expressed
and my many old tales

When I stopped for food
dipped my feet within
it cooled them a little
refreshing my mood

As all friendships do
in time and progression
our paths moved away
as we ended our session

I said my goodbyes
reluctantly waved
took the track to the town
where my road was paved

At nights as I sleep
I sometimes return
to my friend the river
with news and concerns

You can speak out loud or temper your conversation to a mere exchange of thoughts. Either way the wilderness can offer many insights that assist with life's journey.

First and Last

When was my
      first swim?
My father's arms
      would have held me

I do recall
      my first horse ride
The horse was friendly
      but in charge

What did I love first
      how can I fathom
Somebody may remember
      better than I

It happens
      it seems
Cards of a deck
      played daily

Unknowing, unaware
      each step is a part
Each day a chapter
      of a life

Tumbling forward
      ever forward
Casting and fishing
      taking it in

There is a unknown moment
      that turns like a switch
Undoing begins
      leaving prevails

No more the new
      no fresh arrivals
Unravelling and losing
      taking a leave

The last times are here
      unheeded
Now walking away
      as if of a calling

Best not to know
      mostly its
A creeping sleeping veil
      that lifts and floats

In a world of a thousand
      lights
One more goes off
      but there are more

Then there are not
      little is left
One more first
      awaits

Meanings

How does it all
    come together
Existing accepting
    unknowing

If we pause
    seeking answers
Do we spoil the
    simplicity

Would we like
    if we were told?
The what where and why
    of truths

Are we on that level
    mentally?
Are we ready
    in courage?

It is a fearsome thing
    this tiny part
We play in some greater purpose
    that has us exist

Some invent their answers
    in silly gods
and hopeless beings
    trapping the unseeing

Outside the blank walls of that
    contained within
Feeling for a power
    we do not have

It will not be for me
    to know
Or generations
    to follow

Our worthiness is
    obviously short
We are far from the gate
    to our universe

Wisdom

It comes by way of stealth
yet known and understood
that where we are and stand
is brief - an interlude

Laying down the ways
the paths the course the news
all the getting all the choices
meanings in the clues

Gathering by chance by ways
some by plans and schoolings
taking all the pieces now
creating lifes slow learning

Never sure of what is gained
experience adds the layers
being part of everyday
meeting other players

So your years increase
horizons multiply
onward through existence
seeing through the lies

The parts the whole
give the rights to know
many answers and ideas
for you in time to show

It is a thankless task
this holding of the flame
all the while you understand
it is a temporary game

You pass on some to others
divulge your inner stores
of pieces and puzzles
of hidden secret laws

Oh how human it is
to be a holder of hopes
storing in a process
the details and the scope

Tripping falling
through it all
becoming wise in any way
that suits the day

It must finish
sadly after all
the storage is elusive
it awaits the fall

Then it happens
all this wealth
is gone too soon forgotten
as if by stealth

End

I see no way
to accept the day
when your end is called
by unknown forces

Do not lay down
do not submit
grow anger at
the taking of your crown

Fight for it all
question the summons
stand up stand tall
make them explain

It is your right
to demand to know
the reasons why
they want you so

Say yet more
for reasons kind
the universe the law
shall hear your roar

Damn them curse them
hit low and foul
heed not their toll
you own your soul

If it fails
if they succeed
then face their face
and damn their need

You may go
to join their call
your cause was just
you gave it all

Universe 1

They played their tunes
Sang words and made songs
Practiced their skills and prepared
For the hour they knew would come
To dance at the gates of eternity

Ribbons and frills and bouquets
Ancient light from the stellar past
Covered their stage of hope
Giving more to the mystery
Than answers that could not be known

Looking out and away to it all
Seeking the steps of their gods
These false idols of their fears
Which have no place to inhabit the mass
That calls its home infinity

Thoughts abound with mighty ideas
Dared by imaginings and possibles
But it is all just fanciful gesturing
That cant be found while earthly bound
To this home that stands alone

The learned ones speak well of it
With thoughts of empty vast accord
Hailing what they find as truth
When it could be skewed in any way
You care to make of it

A last minute addition.
Written when I had doubts
about our species.
These doubts remain.

Universe 2

Existence is a massive risk
A chance from which they drew a win
But this prize has rules of consequence
Fleeting parts and complex times
Tricks that leave the players out

These humans are but a growth of cells
Found or lost on a tiny outpost of nothing
At the edge of no place else

When they go as go they must
It will be but the faintest flicker in the universe

PHOTO CREDITS

Creators of the originals images

Page 10	Unknown	'In The Dark'
Page 16	Neil Stanners	'Off The Track'
Page 20	Marius Matusc	'Bus Stop'
Page 24	Neil Stanners	'Southern Winter Morning'
Page 28	Public domain	'Crossing Holy Loch'
Page 31	Neil Stanners	'Hokum Skokum'
Page 36	Neil Stanners	'A Loss'
Page 40	Neil Stanners	'Home Town Visit'
Page 42	Arek Socha	'Voyagers'
Page 46	Neil Stanners	'Silence and Summer Heat;
Page 48/49	Neil Stanners	'A Bush Clearing'
Page 52	Neil Stanners	'Landfall'
Page 55	Calo Lisa	'Softly'
Page 62	Public domain	'The Last Words Of Moorant'
Page 64	Public domain	'Autumn On Bayswater Road'
Page 68	Nerrisa J	'Empty Road'
Page 74	Martha Doming	'Sister Carey's Loss'
Page 78	Anne Nygard	'Photos'
Page 80	Neil Stanners	'The Kid'
Page 82	Neil Stanners	'The Other One'
Page 88	Neil Stanners	'The Poem'
Page 92	Martin Dorsch	'The Travellers Tale'
Page 94	Adiel Kloppen	"Beach'
Page 98	Unknown	'Black'
Page 106	Snowscat	'End'

www.ingramcontent.com/pod-product-compliance
Lightning Source LLC
Chambersburg PA
CBHW051333110526
44591CB00026B/2991